The Lost Railways of Yorkshire's N
Neil Burgess

© Neil Burgess, 2011
First published in the United Kingdom, 2011,
by Stenlake Publishing Ltd.
www.stenlake.co.uk
01290 551122
ISBN 9781840335552

Printed by
Blissetts, Roslin Road, Acton, W3 8DH

The publishers regret that they cannot supply
copies of any pictures featured in this book.

Levisham Station.

Acknowledgements

Once again, my thanks are due to my friend and fellow railway historian Richard Morton for his careful checking of the main text of this book. As a Yorkshireman he has a particular reason for ensuring that the history of lines in his native county are properly represented.

The publishers wish to thank the following for contributing photographs to this book: John Alsop for the front and back covers, the inside back cover, pages 2, 4, 6, 7, 8, 9, 12, 14, 15, 16, 17, 18, 19, 21, 22, 24, 25, 26, 27, 28, 29, 30, 31, 32, 33, 34, 35, 36, 37, 38, 39, 40, 42, 43, 44, 45, 46, 47, 48, 49, 50, 51, 52, 53, 55, and 56 (both); and Richard Casserley for pages 1, 5, 10, 11, 13, and 54.

INTRODUCTION

The North Riding of Yorkshire contains a rich diversity of scenery and locations. In the south is the Vale of York, with its gently undulating landscape, which gives way as one moves northeastwards to the coast from regal Scarborough to picturesque Whitby. The high sea cliffs and the small villages like Robin Hood's Bay, which huddle beneath them, lead on, as one travels westwards inland, to the spectacular remoteness of the moors around Goathland and Grosmont. Moving further north, towards the Tees, lies Cleveland, one of the important ironstone extracting areas of the nineteenth-century industrial revolution. Until its separation from the historic North Riding in 1974, Cleveland provided an industrial counterpoint to the predominantly rural areas further south and west. Indeed, just across the boundary in County Durham was the very cradle of public steam-operated railways, the Stockton & Darlington.

The railways of the North Riding were as diverse as the landscapes they crossed. The main line between York and Newcastle ran through almost level country, giving the North Eastern Railway a stretch of main line as fast as any on the East Coast route to Scotland. The coastal line from Scarborough to Whitby, by contrast, hugged the cliff tops and abounded in sharp curves and steep gradients, making it a particular problem for operators, who also had to contend with sea fogs and other hazards of nature. The line north of Pickering up to Grosmont threaded its way through the moorland valleys, passing through countryside more or less inaccessible to road traffic even today. In the high moorland bounded by County Durham to the east and Westmoreland to the west, the line from Barnard Castle to Tebay saw trains of coke and iron slogging across the Pennines, striding across deep valleys on slender wrought-iron viaducts. In the moorland north of comfortable Harrogate, branch lines pushed their way into the high hills through Swaledale to Richmond and through Wensleydale to join up with the Midland Railway's Settle – Carlisle line.

Outside of Cleveland the North Riding, like the East Riding, was and still is predominantly a rural area, dependent mainly on various branches of agriculture, and latterly on tourism. In such country railways, being particularly suited to carrying the bulky products of industry, tended to struggle for existence rather than thrive. Even so, many of the lines which succumbed to rationalisation during the post-war period had sustained a long fight for survival and no doubt served the communities along their way as best they could. Though such fascinating byways as the Sand Hutton and the Easingwold have disappeared long ago, the North Riding has a fair share of secondary routes given a new lease of life as heritage lines such as the Wensleydale branch which reopened during the 1990s. However, the premier steam railway in this part of England must be the North Yorkshire Moors line between Pickering and Grosmont, reopened during the 1970s and firmly fixed in the tourist itinerary by its association with the long-running television series *Heartbeat*. The NYMR not only has one of the longest routes of a preserved line in the country, but runs through spectacular moorland. The recent extension of operations to include services over the national network from Grosmont to Whitby marks a new phase in the history of preserved lines in Britain. Steam is also to be seen regularly between York and Scarborough, and York itself is home to the National Railway Museum.

Survivals from the historic past may delight both the tourist and railway enthusiast but lines through the North Riding still form an important part of the national railway network. The York – Darlington section of the East Coast main line is the most obvious of these, but routes to Scarborough, Whitby and Leeds carry not only extensive passenger traffic but in some cases also a large volume of freight. There is still plenty of life in the North Riding's railways, even though much has gone.

Alne — Easingwold

Passenger service withdrawn	29 November 1948
Distance	2½ miles
Company	Easingwold Railway
Stations closed	*Date of closure*
Easingwold	29 November 1948

Easingwold Station.

Easingwold is a country market town and the York & Newcastle Railway was authorised to build a line to it from Raskelf on the York – Darlington route as early as 1847. Nothing came of this and it was left to local initiative to promote and build a railway, which opened on 27 July 1891. The junction with the east coast line was at Alne, two and half miles away and there were no intermediate stations.

The Easingwold Railway was one of those small lines which attract an interest disproportionate to their size from railway enthusiasts, though local travellers are often lukewarm about their charms. It was operated by a single locomotive, from 1903 the Hudswell, Clarke six-coupled saddle-tank *Easingwold*, which was numbered 2 in the company's stock since it displaced an earlier locomotive. Two four-wheeled passenger coaches, obtained second-hand from the North Eastern, made up most trains, which tended to run 'mixed' with goods wagons marshalled at the rear.

The 11.00 a.m. train to Alne at Easingwold, 30 June 1933.

Later, a former North London Railway four-wheeler and a six-wheeled vehicle from the Great Central Railway swelled their ranks. In 1910 there were nine return journeys on weekdays, often connecting with main-line trains at Alne; by 1946 this had shrunk to two between Monday and Friday with an extra on Saturdays. When *Easingwold* was indisposed, the company hired engines from the North Eastern and later the LNER, and eventually the local engine succumbed completely, leaving the hirelings to run the line.

The company was never absorbed into any other, nor nationalised in 1948. Somehow it maintained a passenger service until 1948, though in the previous year it carried an average of twelve passengers a week with ticket sales for the year amounting to a mere £18. Goods continued until 27 December 1957. In later years the line became popular with enthusiasts and the last passenger-carrying train, which ran in the summer of 1957, conveyed up to three hundred people in open goods wagons.

Barnard Castle — Middleton-in-Teesdale *

Passenger service withdrawn	30 November 1964
Distance	8¾ miles
Company	Tees Valley Railway

Stations closed	Date of closure
Cotherstone **	30 November 1964
Romaldkirk	30 November 1964
Mickleton	30 November 1964
Middleton-in-Teesdale ***	30 November 1964

* The closed station on this line that was in County Durham was Barnard Castle.
** Renamed Cotherston on 1 January 1906 but reverted to its original name in April 1914.
*** Originally named Middleton until June 1894.

Romaldkirk Station, *c. 1914.*

Following the opening of the South Durham & Lancashire Union Railway west of Barnard Castle in 1861, a further local company promoted a short branch line from Tees Valley Junction up to Middleton-in-Teesdale. The line's main purpose was to provide transport for stone quarried beyond Middleton and it opened to traffic on 12 May 1868. Initially there were stations at Cotherstone and Mickleton, Romaldkirk opening two months after the line. The local company operated the line until 1882 when it was absorbed by the North Eastern Railway.

Middleton-in-Teesdale Station, *c.* 1930.

The quarries along the route were connected to the branch by private lines, mostly standard gauge, though Lunedale Quarry, between Mickleton and Middleton, operated a 2 feet, 9 inch gauge line to exchange sidings controlled by Lunedale Quarry signal box. Middleton, Park End and Crossthwaite quarries were all in the immediate area of Middleton Station. Middleton Quarry closed around 1930 and Crossthwaite sent most of its production out by road from 1952. A further quarry at Greengates closed in 1917. In 1914 work started on the construction of a reservoir at Grassholme and sidings were provided for transfer of materials to the works from Mickleton.

An engine shed was provided at Middleton and most trains in the twentieth century worked beyond Barnard Castle to Darlington. There were five trains a day each way in 1922 and in 1946 this had increased to six, with one return journey on Sunday evenings. As with most rural lines passenger traffic was never heavy, goods providing most of the revenue. Steam traction ceased for passenger workings in 1957, the shed at Middleton closing at the same time, and multiple unit diesel trains took over. The line managed to survive the closure of the Stainmore route in 1962, retaining its passenger service until 30 November 1964. Goods traffic lingered on until 5 April the following year and two years later, in 1967, the track was lifted. The route of the line is now a walkers' path and the intermediate stations have been converted to dwellings.

Battersby — Picton

Passenger service withdrawn	14 June 1954	*Stations closed*	*Date of closure*
Distance	12¼ miles	Stokesley	14 June 1954
Company	North Yorkshire & Cleveland Railway	Sexhow	14 June 1954
		Potto	14 June 1954
Stations closed	*Date of closure*	Trenholme Bar	14 June 1954
Ingleby	14 June 1954	Picton	4 January 1960

This was a section of a route intended to tap the reserves of iron ore in the upper Esk Valley and thereby to link Whitby to Stockton, via Grosmont and Picton. Promoted by the North Yorkshire & Cleveland Railway, it was absorbed by the North Eastern in 1859 before all of it opened to traffic. Further lines were planned and construction work on one from Brotton to Leaholme Moor was started, but the ironstone gave out and the project was abandoned.

Without mineral traffic the line was not heavily used and in 1910 there was a service of six trains a day in each direction over it, running from Whitby to Stockton. Some trains reversed at Battersby to serve Middlesborough. In 1946 the service was down to four trains a day Mondays to Fridays and seven on Saturdays, with no Sunday service. Rationalisation in the 1950s saw the closure to passengers of the Battersby to Picton section in 1954, necessitating the reversal of all trains at Battersby in order to get to and from Middlesborough.

The line between Picton and Stokesley closed completely from 1 December 1958, the Stokesley – Battersby section continuing until 2 August 1965. Stokesley Station had its moment of fame before closure when it featured in the 1952 British Transport Film Unit documentary *Farmer Moving South*, about a complete farm removal from Stokesley to Hartfield in Sussex, on the former London, Brighton & South Coast line from East Grinstead to Tunbridge Wells.

Stokesley Station.

Darlington — Tebay: 'The Stainmore Line' *

Passenger service withdrawn 14 June 1954
Distance 51¼ miles
Company
Darlington — Barnard Castle:
Darlington & Barnard Castle Railway
Barnard Castle — Tebay:
South Durham & Lancashire Union Railway

Stations closed — *Date of closure*
Lartington — 22 January 1962
Bowes — 22 January 1962

* Closed passenger stations on this line that were in County Durham were Piercebridge, Gainford, Winston, Broomielaw and Barnard Castle (both stations). Closed stations on the line that were in Westmoreland were Barras, Kirkby Stephen, Smardale, Ravenstonedale and Gaisgill.

Bowes Station.

Northern England was home to much of the large-scale iron and steel making in the years before the Great War, though the main areas of production, in northeast Yorkshire and County Durham, and in Cumberland, Westmoreland and north Lancashire, were separated by the inhospitable country of the northern Pennines. With the advent of the railway age there came the possibility of a means of moving coke and iron ore between the two which could negotiate the uplands as canals could not.

In 1854 an Act of Parliament authorised the construction of the first stage of a railway from Darlington to the west and the Darlington & Barnard Castle Railway was opened on 8 July 1856 between those towns. In the following year a line was authorised west of Barnard Castle to cross the high moorland to Kirkby Stephen and Tebay, the latter a point on the Lancaster & Carlisle Railway at the foot of the great incline to Shap, and from there on to the Scottish border. The South Durham & Lancashire Union Railway was a protégé of the renowned Stockton & Darlington Railway, still an independent company, and its engineer, Thomas Bouch, was the brother of the Stockton & Darlington's locomotive superintendent, William Bouch.

The line was from the first primarily a mineral carrier; passenger traffic from the remote moors was never likely to be profitable, though those making the journey over the years would be rewarded – on fine days at least – with views of country spectacular enough to delight the heart of any Victorian romantic. Given the difficult terrain, construction work was surprisingly rapid, the line opening to mineral traffic on 4 July 1861. The high moors were cut by deep valleys which Bouch managed to cross using not only conventional stone viaducts, as at Smardale, but also on very attractive structures of wrought and cast iron at Deepdale and Belah. The iron structures not only looked light and graceful, but were surprisingly strong and were also relatively inexpensive to build. They established their creator's reputation for such engineering feats which ultimately, and in the end tragically, led to his gaining the contract to design the ill-fated first Tay Bridge. Bouch's reputation collapsed with his bridge and inevitably anxiety was expressed over the safety of Belah and Deepdale but such fears proved groundless and they remained in use until the line closed in 1962.

Bowes Station, 4 September 1955.

The final section of railway, between Kirkby Stephen and Penrith, was authorised in 1858 and opened in April 1862 for mineral traffic and two months later for passengers. In due course, when the Midland Railway drove its line from Settle Junction to Carlisle in 1876, a connection between the two routes was made at Appleby. In its traverse of the Pennines the line reached 1,370 feet above sea level at Stainmore summit, one of the highest in England. For a century an endless succession of mineral trains, carrying coke from Durham and iron ore from Workington, plodded and blasted their way up the gradients and over the barren moors. In summer excursions were run to and from Blackpool and other northwestern resorts, though purely local traffic was always sparse. The weather could be atrocious and heavy falls of snow might bring the line to a standstill for days or even weeks. In 1955 one such incident was made into the subject of a British Transport Film Unit documentary, *Snowdrift at Bleath Gill*, which gives a sense of the struggle involved in keeping such lines open.

It was not the weather, though, which ended the life of the Stainmore line. The passenger service from Kirkby Stephen to Tebay ended in 1952 and the whole route west of Barnard Castle closed ten years later. The section back to Darlington went two years later, the line effectively contracting in the opposite order to that of its building. Bouch's iron viaducts were demolished, leaving just the stone abutments at either end, eighty years after their designer's humiliation and early death; their long service should have done something to redeem his reputation. Gone the line may be, but it certainly has not been forgotten.

Eryholme — Richmond

Passenger service withdrawn   3rd March 1969
Distance   9¾ miles
Company   Great North of England Railway

Stations closed	Date of closure
Moulton	3 March 1969
Scorton	3 March 1969
Catterick Bridge	3 March 1969
Richmond	3 March 1969

Moulton Station, 3 September 1956.

During the nineteenth century Richmond was a long-established market town at the head of Swaledale, an area known not only for agriculture but also lead mining. Its importance was emphasised when the Great North of England Railway obtained an Act of Parliament on 21 July 1845 to construct a line from Dalton Junction, on the main line from York to Newcastle, to the town, which opened to traffic from 10 September the following year. Though small, the station building was attractive and became a much-admired local landmark. Dalton Junction was renamed Eryholme in May 1901.

Scorton Station.

The Richmond branch would, in all probability, have remained a peaceful country byway like other lines in the North Riding and elsewhere had not international events imposed themselves. The outbreak of the Great War in 1914 saw a considerable need for areas to billet and train troops and the wide expanses of the North Riding were thought ripe for use. A camp was established at Catterick, two miles south of Richmond, and during the war a steeply-graded four-mile branch line was constructed by the War Department from Catterick Bridge Station to serve it. Catterick became one of the great army centres throughout the twentieth century and the many thousands of soldiers stationed there arrived and left by train until 1964, when the camp branch closed for passenger traffic. The continuation of conscription after 1945 ensured that countless men on National Service became acquainted with this short section of railway. In addition the Army used an assortment of requisitioned locomotives and rolling stock over the line. There were accidents, the most serious of which occurred on 4 February 1944 when ammunition being loaded at Catterick Bridge exploded, killing twelve people including the stationmaster and two female railway clerks.

4-6-2T No. 69834 with the 8.42 a.m. train to Darlington at Richmond Station, 3 September 1956.

The Richmond branch service ran mainly to and from Darlington, often in the hands of North Eastern 0-4-4 tank engines, originally BTPs and class A, latterly class O (LNER class G5). Larger engines were used on military trains, including 4-6-2 tanks of LNER class A5, which were used in pairs over the camp line because of the gradients. In later days, multiple-unit diesel trains took over the workings.

The branch did not long outlive the closure of the line to the army camp, passenger services ending on 3 March 1969 with goods, mainly to Catterick Bridge, following on 9 February 1970. Station buildings and associated houses remain, the house at Catterick Bridge still bearing the scars of the 1944 disaster.

Gilling — Malton

Passenger service withdrawn	1 January 1931	*Stations closed*	*Date of closure*
Distance	13 miles	Barton-le-Street †	1 January 1931
Company	York, Newcastle & Berwick Railway	Amotherby †	1 January 1931

† Passenger services withdrawn in 1931 but remained open on a restricted basis until final closure after 26 June 1958.

* Originally named Hovingham until 1 October 1896.

Stations closed	*Date of closure*
Hovingham Spa † *	1 January 1931
Slingsby †	1 January 1931

Slingsby Station.

Slingsby Station, *c.* **1917.**

This section of the York, Newcastle & Berwick line from Pilmoor was opened with the section to Gilling in May 1853 (see the section on Pilmoor – Pickering) as part of the route from Scarborough to the northeast and Scotland. Despite this intention, it was never possible to travel through Malton directly to the coast, trains requiring to reverse into the station from Scarborough Road Junction with the train engine still attached to the rear – only then could they proceed. Such an operational difficulty on a line never conceived of as a through route, allied to the construction of the line from Gilling to Pickering and thence to Scarborough, consigned it to secondary status. Even so, the timetable in 1910 indicates a service of five trains each way daily to and from Pilmoor, more than on the Gilling – Pickering section. However, trains from Malton tended to run to York via Pilmoor while those from Pickering connected at Gilling with services to York.

Barton-le-Street Station.

The line closed to passengers from the first day of 1931, the Depression probably removing what little profitability remained. There was a serious derailment at Pilmoor on 19 March 1963 which badly damaged the junction and it was decided not to repair it. By this time services using the line were limited to a pick-up goods train for Malton which ran for the last time on 7 August 1964, though a contract to supply the flour mill at Amotherby saw trains to there continue until 16 October.

Grosmont — Beck Hole

Passenger service withdrawn 21 September 1914
Distance 1 mile
Company Whitby & Pickering Railway

Stations closed	Date of closure
Beck Holes	1 July 1865
Beck Hole *	21 September 1914

* Replaced Beck Holes when the line was realigned on its new formation.

Beck Hole Station.

This very short line's existence as a piece of railway separate and distinct from the rest of the Whitby & Pickering Railway dates from the construction and opening in 1865 of a diversion from the original route intended to avoid the need for the rope-worked incline between Grosmont and Goathland. However, there is some debate about precisely what provision was made for passengers in the early days; there seems to have been a station of some sort at the foot of the incline and it is mentioned in official documents in 1859, but in all probability it was a rudimentary structure which came into being as a result of the need to halt trains at the foot of the incline to attach or detach them from the haulage rope. There were, at various times, at least two incumbents of the office of station master; but the opening of the deviation saw the closure of the old line south of Beck Hole and the cessation of passenger services northwards to Deviation Junction, Grosmont, where the new line took its leave of the original route.

The hamlet of Beck Hole was, until very recent times, an isolated place with difficult road access down steep hills. The railway remained in use for goods traffic, including the short-lived iron works, and in the early years of the twentieth century the area became popular with summer visitors keen to sample the bracing air of the moorland. By this time railway companies were experimenting with more economical forms of operation than hitherto and the idea of the 'push-pull' or 'motor' train had gained acceptance as an ideal type for less well-used lines. Thus it was that in 1908 the North Eastern Railway built a second passenger station at Beck Hole and operated a service from Whitby via Grosmont using such a train – or 'autocar' as the company preferred to call it – comprising a tank engine and a trailer car. The new Beck Hole Station was mainly aimed at encouraging tourists and sources claim it operated only during the summer months of July, August and September. The station building was virtually at ground level and tickets were issued by the guard of the autocar. The service continued until the end of the summer timetable of 1914, when it was suspended as a wartime measure, never to be reinstated. Goods services continued until 1952, though the branch suffered progressive contraction over the years as the industries it served declined and disappeared. The route of the line is now part of the 'Rail Trail' walking path between Grosmont and Goathland.

Harrogate — Northallerton *

Passenger service withdrawn — 6 March 1967
Distance — 28¼ miles
Company — Leeds & Thirsk Railway

Stations closed — Date of closure
Melmerby ** — 6 March 1967
Sinderby — 1 January 1962
Pickhill — 14 September 1959
Newby Wiske *** — 11 September 1939

* Closed passenger stations on this line that were in the West Riding were Nidd Bridge, Wormald Green and Ripon.
** Originally named Wath until February 1852.
*** Originally closed on 20 September 1915 but later reopened (date unknown). The last train ran in 1939 with official closure not coming until 2 September 1946.

Melmerby Station.

In 1844 a prospectus was issued for a line between Leeds and Thirsk, intending to make a direct northward link onto the York to Darlington line. Powers were granted by an act of 21 July 1845 and work commenced on 20 October in the same year, services between Ripon and Thirsk beginning from 1 June 1848. Meanwhile a railway from Melmerby to Northallerton was first proposed in 1845 as an extension of the Leeds & Thirsk line, aiming to join the Stockton & Hartlepool Railway at Billingham. Pressure from George Hudson led to the temporary abandonment of the scheme. Hudson's departure from the scene allowed a reconsideration of the idea and in 1848 powers were granted for a Melmerby to Northallerton line, which eventually opened on 2 June 1852.

Pickhill Station.

However, the plan to run directly from Leeds to Stockton was thwarted for a further three and a half years until a connection between the Leeds Northern Railway (as the Leeds & Thirsk had become) and the Great North of England line at Thirsk was laid in. When they did so trains ran via Thirsk and it was 1901 before the Melmerby to Northallerton section was doubled and became the main route, the Melmerby to Thirsk line declining in importance. The layout at Northallerton allowed trains from Leeds to pass under the main York to Darlington route so a connecting spur was laid from Cordio Junction to give access to the main line station, the platforms on the Melmerby line becoming disused. The North Eastern had planned to build a marshalling yard at Northallerton in the early years of the twentieth century, but nothing came of it. Thus Northallerton remained a moderately important junction station, but the line from Harrogate declined over the years, a process aided by the widening of the East Coast line in 1959 which reduced the need for a diversionary route, and closure came in 1967, the wayside stations closing even earlier. A brief renaissance occurred when a serious accident south of Thirsk, in which a Cliff – Uddingstone cement train became derailed and the wreckage was hit by an express hauled by the prototype English Electric diesel DP2, completely blocked the East Coast line. Down traffic was routed over the Northallerton – Ripon section until the wreckage was removed and the main line reopened on 2 August.

It was a sad end for a route which, until 1964, had been used by Liverpool – Newcastle expresses and was the means by which the *Queen of Scots* Pullman express from King's Cross to Glasgow had regained the East Coast main line after diverting westwards at Doncaster to serve Harrogate; a circuitous way of getting to Scotland which may have been compensated for by the luxury of Pullman travel. Now both the line and the *Queen of Scots* have passed into history.

Knaresborough — Pilmoor *

Passenger service withdrawn	25 September 1950
Distance	13 ¼ miles
Company	York & Newcastle Railway (but see text)

Stations closed	Date of closure
Boroughbridge (1st station)	1 April 1875
Boroughbridge (2nd station) **	25 September 1950
Brafferton	25 September 1950
Pilmoor	5 May 1958

* The closed passenger station on this line that was in the West Riding was Copgrove.
** Replaced the first station when the line was extended.

This is a fairly short section of railway with a long and complex history. The line was built in two sections, the first of which, from the York to Darlington main line at Pilmoor to Boroughbridge, was authorised by Parliament in 1846. Promotion of the line was in the hands of the Great North of England Railway, but hardly was the ink on the Act dry than the GNofER was absorbed by the Newcastle & Darlington Junction Railway, which thereupon became transformed into the York & Newcastle Railway. The line had originally been intended to reach Harrogate and had been planned in 1843, but the proposal was shelved as one of George Hudson's many manoeuvres and the line foreshortened to go only as far as Boroughbridge. In this form the six miles of railway opened to traffic on 17 June 1847, though there is some doubt whether Pilmoor was actually ready for use at this date.

The next proposal to go beyond Boroughbridge was a line approaching from the south, linking the York & North Midland line from Church Fenton to Harrogate at Pannal with the Pilmoor to Boroughbridge section. Hudson again caused the abandonment of the scheme, but this time indirectly, since the time of financial stringency occasioned by his downfall meant there was no money to build it. Then in 1865 a further plan, this time for a direct Leeds to Scarborough route using the Boroughbridge – Pilmoor – Malton lines, was proposed. This was curtailed as an economy, only the Knaresborough to Boroughbridge section being built and opening to traffic from 1 April 1875, including a new station to replace the original at Boroughbridge, which was turned over to goods traffic. At Pilmoor a connection bridging the East Coast line was built but never used.

The line ran through a predominantly agricultural area and transported produce out and supplies of animal feed, fertilisers and coal in. As with other rural lines in this book, and many more throughout the country, it was hard put to compete with road transport in the inter-war period and economies, including a signalling system based on fixed and moving warning boards rather than conventional semaphore signals, failed to save it. In 1910 there were five return journeys a day covering the whole line, trains running to and from Harrogate, with one return trip from Harrogate to Boroughbridge. By 1946 this had become two return journeys each weekday, with an extra train on Tuesdays between Harrogate and Brafferton and four return trips on Saturdays. It cannot have been a surprise to anyone that passenger services ended on 25 September 1950. The original section of line between Pilmoor and Boroughbridge was closed completely at the same time, leaving the Knaresborough – Boroughbridge section to soldier on as a goods-only line until 5 October 1964.

Malton — Grosmont

Passenger service withdrawn	8 March 1965
Distance	28¾ miles
Company	Whitby & Pickering Railway

Stations closed	*Date of closure*
Marishes Road *	8 March 1965
Pickering **	8 March 1965
Levisham ***	8 March 1965
Newton Dale ****	After September 1948
Goathland (1st station) †	1 July 1865
Goathland (2nd station) ††	8 March 1965

* Originally named High Marishes; renamed by July 1848.
** Reopened on the North Yorkshire Moors Railway on 29 March 1975.
*** Reopened on the North Yorkshire Moors Railway on 22 April 1973.
**** Reopened as Newtondale Halt on the North Yorkshire Moors Railway.
† Replaced by the second station when the line was realigned.
†† Originally named Goathland Mill until 1 November 1891. Reopened on the North Yorkshire Moors Railway on 22 April 1973.

Marishes Road Station, January 1911.

Goathland (2nd) Station.

This section of railway was virtually the first to be constructed in the North Riding and appropriately was engineered by George Stephenson. Obtaining its Act of Parliament in 1833 and opening from Whitby to Grosmont in June 1835 and to Pickering on 26 May 1836, it was originally worked by horses for most of its distance, with a rope-worked inclined plane between Grosmont and Goathland, built on a gradient of 1 in 15. Although there were many such inclines in the northeast of England serving collieries, this one conveyed loaded passenger trains as well. The incline was a water-balance type, the ascending vehicles' weight being counteracted by a tank wagon filled with water at the top and emptied at the foot of the gradient. Water balance inclines still exist in several locations – the one between the villages of Lynton and Lynmouth in north Devon being possibly the best known – but efficient braking is a necessity and this the early examples lacked. The North Eastern Railway, which by then had assumed responsibility for the line and converted the more easily graded sections to locomotive haulage from 1847, set about replacing the incline with a more easily graded route worked by locomotives, in the meantime replacing the water-balance system with a steam winding engine. However, before the new line opened in 1865 two passengers were killed in an accident caused by the breakage of the haulage rope and the subsequent runaway of the train.

The replacement of the incline led to alterations to the line. The tunnel south of Grosmont Station was replaced by one of larger cross-section to allow locomotives to pass through it; the original tunnel was converted to be used by pedestrians. The line was realigned at Goathland and a new station opened on the new section. However, the old incline still had some useful life in it and the track was relaid in 1872 by the Leeds locomotive builders Manning, Wardle to try out some locomotives built to use the Fell principle of adhesion – involving additional wheels gripping a central rail between the running rails – which it had built for a railway in Brazil. Even after the incline itself was abandoned, the railway to the foot of it remained *in situ* until 1951, a fortnightly goods train running to serve several remote cottages; before the Great War there had even been a service of passenger trains for holidaymakers.

Goathland (2nd) Station, *c.* 1912.

Although situated today in a national park and being very rural, some heavy industry was to be found along the line. Ironworks were built at Beck Hole and Grosmont during the 1860s, the former having a very short life but the latter lasting until the 1890s. Seasonal passenger traffic, mainly to Whitby, was always significant, though in 1910 the regular service between Malton and Whitby was six trains each way on weekdays and one return trip on Sundays. The summer timetable for 1947 had five return weekday trains and the Sunday service had gone altogether.

The Beeching economies of the 1960s were particularly assiduous in seeking out routes with mainly seasonal usage and the line from Malton to its junction with the Esk Valley line at Grosmont was one such. Closure as a through route came in 1965, but this was not to be the end. From 1973 the line from Pickering northwards was reopened as the North Yorkshire Moors Railway, which has become one of Britain's premier restored lines and probably carries far more passengers today than at any time in its history. The 1 in 49 gradient up to Goathland still taxes the largest of locomotives and is one of the steepest on any standard gauge preserved line. In the latter part of the twentieth century the area around Goathland and Grosmont was used for filming the television series *Heartbeat* and its popularity has added to the appeal of the line. There seems every possibility that George Stephenson's line through the moors has a long life ahead of it.

Melmerby — Masham

Passenger service withdrawn	1 January 1931
Distance	7¾ miles
Company	North Eastern Railway

Stations closed	Date of closure
Tanfield	1 January 1931
Masham	1 January 1931

Tanfield Station.

In 1865 an Act was passed giving powers for a scheme to construct a railway from Hawes in Wensleydale to Melmerby on the Northallerton – Harrogate line. Nothing came of the plan and the powers lapsed. The prospect of an independent line entering its territory unnerved the North Eastern and, in the hope of forestalling another incursion into the area, it promoted its own line from Melmerby northwestwards to Masham. The line was seven miles long and had a single intermediate station at Tanfield. Authorised in 1871, it opened for traffic on 9 June 1875 and there was little prospect of generating much traffic beyond the usual agricultural offerings and a limited number of passengers. In 1910 these had been conveyed on four return workings each weekday, trains running to and from Ripon.

Masham Station, late nineteenth century.

The uplands of Colsterdale around Masham were selected as sites for reservoirs to supply Leeds and Harrogate and the early decades of the twentieth century saw a good deal of construction traffic pass over the branch, being forwarded beyond the terminus by a narrow-gauge light railway, which closed in 1926 and was dismantled in 1932. It might be argued that this was in fact two railways in one, since gauges of both 2 feet and 3 feet were employed. In connection with its New Leighton Reservoir, Leeds Corporation built a village for the construction workers and their families at Breary Banks and this was turned over to the War Office during the Great War for use as an army camp. From 1917 until the end of the war it was used to house German prisoners of war before being returned to civilian accommodation until the completion of the construction project. Harrogate's reservoir was at Roundhill, not far from New Leighton. Once the last of the reservoirs was completed in 1926 traffic on the branch fell off again and passenger services succumbed as early as the first day of 1931. The Second World War saw the area used for the storage of ammunition before D-Day and this gave a further boost to goods traffic which eventually managed to outlive the passenger workings by more than three decades, ending finally on 11 November 1963.

Melmerby — Masham

Melmerby — Thirsk

Passenger service withdrawn	14 September 1959	* Renamed Baldersby Gate between July 1855 and April 1863.
Distance	6 miles	** Renamed Topcliffe Gate between July 1854 and April 1863.
Company	Leeds & Thirsk Railway	*** Originally named Thirsk Town; renamed in June 1852. It became a goods depot after closure to passenger services.

Stations closed	Date of closure
Baldersby*	14 September 1959
Topcliffe **	14 September 1959
Thirsk ***	December 1855

Baldersby Station, *c.* 1906.

Topcliffe Station, *c.* 1910.

The origins of this line as part of the Leeds & Thirsk Railway have already been mentioned in connection with the Harrogate to Northallerton line. Authorised in 1848 and opened in June of the same year with the Leeds & Thirsk line south of Melmerby, this six-mile section was used as the main route from 1 January 1856 until 1901 because it had a direct connection to the York to Darlington line at Thirsk. After that date its fortunes declined and it became very much the secondary route, though the original station at Thirsk Town was far closer to the centre than the junction on the East Coast route. The North Eastern Railway even operated a bus service between the town and the station until 1914. By 1946 it had a stopping passenger service of only four trains a day in each direction, with two in each direction on Sundays. In latter years only one running line was used, the other being for storage of surplus wagons. It closed from 14 September 1959 and the more favoured route to Northallerton only outlived it by eight years.

Melmerby — Thirsk

Northallerton — Hawes — Garsdale

Passenger service withdrawn	26 April 1954 (but see text)
Distance	39¾ miles
Company	see text

Stations closed	Date of closure
Ainderby	26 April 1954
Scruton *	26 April 1954
Leeming Bar †**	26 April 1954
Bedale †	26 April 1954
Crakehall ***	26 April 1954
Jervaulx ****	26 April 1954
Finghall Lane †	26 April 1954
Constable Burton	26 April 1954
Spennithorne ‡	26 April 1954
Leyburn †	26 April 1954
Wensley	26 April 1954
Redmire ††	26 April 1954
Aysgarth	26 April 1954

Stations closed	Date of closure
Askrigg	26 April 1954
Hawes	16 March 1959
Garsdale ‡‡	4 May 1970

* Originally named Scruton Lane; renaming date unknown.
** Originally named Leeming Lane until 1 July 1902.
*** Closed for an unknown length of time from 1 March 1917 and later reopened.
**** Originally named Newton-Le-Willows until 1 December 1877.
† Reopened on the Wensleydale Railway on 4 July 2003.
†† Reopened on the Wensleydale Railway in August 2004.
‡ Closed between 1 March 1917 and 18 September 1920.
‡‡ Originally named Hawes; renamed Hawes Junction & Garsdale on 20 January 1900 and Garsdale from 1 September 1932. The station was reopened from 14 July 1986, although it may have been used for occasional 'Dalesrail' excursions between 1970 and that date.

Ainderby Station.

Bedale Station, *c.* 1905.

Wensleydale, known by many people only in connection with the cheese made locally, was a goal for railway expansion in the mid-nineteenth century, partly because of local traffic – mainly milk and building stone – but also because it offered an east – west connection through the Pennines. The 39-mile branch through the dale linked the East Coast main line at Northallerton with the Midland Railway's route to Scotland via Leeds, Settle Junction and Carlisle and involved no less than four railway companies in its promotion and construction.

Constable Burton Station.

The first section of line, between Northallerton and Bedale, was originally authorised in the Act for the construction of the Great North of England Railway in April 1846, but by the time it opened to Leeming two years later it was by the York, Newcastle & Berwick Railway, as the GNER's successor. The line was then extended to Leyburn by the Bedale & Leyburn Railway, a predominantly local route supported and paid for by landowners in the area. Goods services began from 24 November 1855 and passenger trains from 19 May the following year. By this time the YN&BR had become one of the constituents of the North Eastern Railway and that company was concerned lest the Bedale & Leyburn fell into the hands of a rival, so it leased the small company from the first day of 1858 and formally absorbed it from 8 August 1859.

Spennithorne Station, *c.* 1908.

The town of Hawes, at the western end of Wensleydale, had been looking for a railway to connect it to the wider world and originally placed its hopes on a line to Wensley and from there, by a connection through Melmerby, to Leeds. Although authorised by Parliament, the line was never built and a cheaper route was sought along the dale to Leyburn and the North Eastern. Authorised on 4 July 1870, it took eight years to construct the sixteen miles, though the section between Leyburn and Askrigg was opened by the North Eastern from 1 February 1877. The first goods trains ran along the whole route on 1 June 1878 with passengers being carried four months later.

Northallerton — Hawes — Garsdale

Askrigg Station, *c.* 1906.

Between the authorisation and opening of the line to Hawes, the Midland Railway had opened its Settle – Carlisle main line through Garsdale to all traffic on 1 May 1876. The Midland and the North Eastern were on amicable terms with one another – possibly helped by having a common rival in the London & North Western – and by the Midland Railway Additional Powers Act of 1875 that company was authorised to construct a five-mile line from a junction with the Settle – Carlisle line to Hawes. Even so, the two companies could not agree on who should run the service along the final section, nor could they come to an amicable arrangement about operating the joint station at Hawes. Their differences delayed the opening of the line, which first saw goods trains on 1 August 1878 and passengers on 1 October the same year. The station at Hawes was jointly owned by the Midland and the North Eastern, so passenger services on either side of Hawes were most likely timed to begin on the same day. Most of the through traffic along the line was worked by the North Eastern, the trains having their own platform face at Hawes Junction along the back of the up main line platform.

Hawes Station, *c.* 1903.

The Wensleydale line lived a relatively uneventful life and after the passenger service between Northallerton and Hawes was withdrawn in 1954, only one return journey remained, which left Garsdale (as Hawes Junction had now become) at 3.16 p.m., returning from Hawes at 4.25. This ended from 16 March 1959, when the line west of Hawes closed entirely. There was a brief return of passenger services during January 1962 when snow threatened to cut off the villages along the dale. Goods traffic continued along the line until 1964 when the entire route west of Redmire was closed completely and the track lifted. Redmire continued to provide stone traffic and an occasional 'Dalesrail' passenger train from York for walkers to explore the dales. General goods traffic ceased in 1982 and the quarry traffic from Redmire ended ten years later.

In the meantime, in 1990, a group had been formed to promote the reopening of the line as a tourist route under the name The Wensleydale Railway. The Ministry of Defence had requested the retention of the line west to Leyburn in order to transport military vehicles to and from Catterick, which helped retain some of the track. The Wensleydale Railway now operates heritage diesel trains between Leeming Bar and Redmire and intends to pursue its aim of reinstating the entire route, which would make it one of the longest heritage lines in the country. There seems to be a future for trains in the dale for a long time yet.

Nunthorpe — Brotton

Passenger service withdrawn	2 March 1964	*Stations closed*	*Date of closure*
Distance	16¾ miles	Hutton Gate **	2 March 1964
Company	**Nunthorpe – Guisborough:**	Guisborough	2 March 1964
	Middlesborough & Guisborough Railway	Boosbeck	2 May 1960
	Hutton Gate – Brotton:		
	Cleveland Railway		

* Originally named Pinchingthorpe, this opened to replace the first station of that name. The spelling of this second station was changed on 1 April 1920.

Stations closed	*Date of closure*
Pinchingthorpe	December 1876
Pinchinthorpe *	29 October 1951

** Closed between May 1864 and July 1881, and between 1 October 1903 and 1 January 1904.

Boosbeck Station.

This route was a further product of the need to transport iron ore from quarries in the Cleveland hills to the iron and steel works of Middlesborough and Stockton-on-Tees. One centre of mining was Guisborough and the period of thirty years from 1850 saw a number of both shaft and drift mines opened which needed rail connections to take away their production. The Middlesborough & Guisborough Railway was authorised by Parliament in 1852 and opened for goods traffic from 11 November 1853, passengers following from February 1854, a good indicator of the priorities which underlay its construction. The route was unexceptional apart from a gradient of 1 in 44 for 1½ miles between Ormesby and Nunthorpe. Guisborough grew to become an important centre for ironstone extraction in Cleveland and other mineral lines were constructed, including one from Battersby to Nunthorpe, opened to goods in 1864 and passengers from 1 April 1868, which made the latter place a junction. The Cleveland Railway constructed a route from Brotton to join up with the M&GR line at Hutton Gate, near Guisborough, which opened on 23 November 1861, though a reversal at Guisborough was needed since the junction faced the wrong way for direct running.

The Middlesborough & Guisborough Railway had close relations with the Stockton & Darlington Railway, which absorbed it in 1857. In 1863 the Stockton & Darlington was itself absorbed into the North Eastern, the Cleveland Railway following suit two years later. In due course the Middlesborough – Guisborough – Brotton line was operated as a connection to Whitby and Scarborough, which gained extra traffic after 1933 when the inland route was preferred over the coastal one through Saltburn. This arrangement ceased from 5 May 1958, and trains to Loftus followed from 2 May 1960, though local traffic continued to Guisborough only until 1964. Today the line eastwards beyond Nunthorpe is no more and trains from Middlesborough reach Whitby through Battersby and Grosmont. Long before this happened, Cleveland ironstone had been replaced for iron and steel making by ores from other parts of Europe, spelling the decline of the local industry.

Pickering — Seamer

Passenger service withdrawn	5 June 1950	*Stations closed*	*Date of closure*
Distance	16¾ miles	Snainton	5 June 1950
Company	North Eastern Railway	Sawdon	5 June 1950
		Wykeham	5 June 1950
Stations closed	*Date of closure*	Forge Valley	5 June 1950
Thornton Dale	5 June 1950		
Ebberston *	5 June 1950	* Originally named Wilton until 1 April 1903.	

Thornton Dale Station.

Ebberston Station, *c.* **1905.**

This line, which ran for much of its length within easy distance of the Scarborough to Pickering road, opened to traffic in 1882 and offered a direct route between the two towns. Unfortunately the proximity to the road, and the distance from the centres of the villages it aimed to serve, meant that it fell prey to the development of rural bus services in the inter-war years. The passenger service in 1910 was of five trains in each direction every weekday, calling at all stations, but without a Sunday service. After the Grouping in 1923 the LNER attempted to reduce costs by using Sentinel geared steam railcars instead of conventional engines and coaches. One of the double-geared Sentinel locomotives was also kept for shunting at Pickering, the intention being that it could deputise for the railcar if it was out of service, the two types being mechanically identical. The railcars could not provide a long-term solution, however, even though the LNER persevered with them for far longer than the LMS; in time they too were replaced with push-pull trains, generally using one of the ubiquitous North Eastern 0-4-4 tanks, which the LNER classified G5. The 1946 summer timetable reveals three trains from Scarborough to Pickering, but four in the opposite direction; a note indicates 'one class only' since the push-pull trains, some of which could consist only of a single coach, had no first class accommodation. Unsurprisingly, the passenger and goods services ceased in 1950, except for the section between Pickering and Thornton Dale which was kept open until 1964, mainly for stone traffic.

Snainton Station.

Given that the line crossed an area which today attracts large numbers of tourists and where roads are becoming increasingly congested, it is easy to say that more foresight might have retained a potentially useful route for the future. Unfortunately, the economics of railway operation in the post-war years could allow no such hypothetical possibilities and the route has reverted to nature. Interestingly, the British Transport Film Unit documentary *This is York*, made in 1953, features a short sequence at Thornton Dale – reputed to be Yorkshire's prettiest village – and makes the comment that consigning traffic by a British Road Services van was offering people a more personal service than the branch train!

Pilmoor — Pickering

Passenger service withdrawn	2 February 1953
Distance	30 miles
Company	
Pilmoor — Gilling:	York, Newcastle & Berwick Railway
Gilling – Pickering:	North Eastern Railway

Stations closed	Date of closure
Husthwaite Gate	2 February 1953
Coxwold *	2 February 1953
Ampleforth	5 June 1950
Gilling **	2 February 1953
Nunnington	2 February 1953
Helmsley	2 February 1953
Nawton	2 February 1953
Kirbymoorside ***	2 February 1953*
Sinnington	2 February 1953

* Remained open on a restricted basis until final closure after June 1958.
** Given the suffix 'for Ampleforth College' in some timetables; remained open on a restricted basis until final closure after 1963.
*** Originally named Kirby Moorside until 31 May 1948.

Husthwaite Gate Station.

Coxwold Station.

For well over a century Pickering was the point of convergence of a pair of routes, one running east – west and the other north – south. The east – west route was originally the most important, its eastern end being built by the York, Newcastle & Berwick Railway, a partner in the Anglo-Scottish main line from London to Edinburgh. The line ran from Pilmoor, on the present-day East Coast route, to Malton, opening on 19 May 1853 and remaining for many years the route by which fares from Scarborough to Darlington were calculated.

Gilling Station, *c.* 1913.

Well into the twentieth century it continued to see expresses from Scarborough to Newcastle and Edinburgh, picking their way along what had by then become a very rural byway; indeed, like many other country lines, it was more useful as a diversionary route for expresses at busy times than as a means of serving the small towns and villages along the way. The Benedictine order of monks had established an abbey and boarding school at Ampleforth during the second half of the nineteenth century and special trains were run to and from Gilling, which was actually nearer to the school than Ampleforth Station itself, at the beginning and end of each term until the line finally closed.

Gilling Station.

Although the York, Berwick & Newcastle route continued beyond Gilling to Malton (see separate section) after the North Eastern Railway built a connection to Pickering this tended to become the main route. The Pickering line was 18¾ miles long, but opened in three sections: the first six miles from Gilling to Helmsley on 9 October 1871; thence to Kirby Moorside on 1 January 1874; and the final section to Pickering on 1 April the following year.

Kirkby Moorside Station, *c.* 1905.

The Gilling – Malton section withered away by 1930, but long before that trains had run directly from York through Pilmoor to Pickering. Even in 1910 there were only four return journeys each weekday, with no Sunday service and by 1947 the frequency had reduced to two trains each way, so closure in 1953 was hardly unexpected (though Ampleforth had closed three years earlier). The passenger service actually ended on 31 January, the day of the great storm which flooded so much of the east coast and badly disrupted rail services further south in Lincolnshire and East Anglia, so perhaps even the elements mourned the line's passing.

Sand Hutton — Scayingham

Passenger service withdrawn	July 1930 *	*Stations closed*	*Date of closure*
Distance	7¼ miles	War Memorial halt	July 1930
Company	Sand Hutton Light Railway	Kissthorne halt	July 1930
		Bossall	July 1930
		Barnby House	July 1930
Stations closed	*Date of closure*		
Warthill **	July 1930		
Sand Hutton	July 1930	* Some sources suggest 1 March 1930.	
Gardens halt	July 1930	** Originally named Stockton; renamed Stockton Forest in April 1867,	
Claxton	July 1930	then Stockton-on-Forest circa 1870, becoming Warthill on 1 February 1872.	

Warthill Station, *c.* 1909.

In the years before the Great War and the development of the internal combustion engine railways were the only effective means of moving passengers and most kinds of goods over even quite modest distances. Several owners of large country estates looked seriously at the possibilities offered by minimum-gauge light railways as internal means of transportation, one of whom was Sir Robert Walker, Bart., of Sand Hutton Hall. His first excursion into an estate railway, in 1912, was a 15-inch gauge line of two miles, operated using a scale model based on an Ivatt large-boilered 'Atlantic' and named *Synolda* after his first wife.

After the Great War, Sir Robert embarked on a more ambitious scheme for a line 7¼ miles long using former War Department equipment, which was readily available at a reasonable price. This entailed regauging the line to 1 foot, 6 inches and it employed four Hunslet 0-4-0 saddle tanks, one of which was named *Esme* after Sir Robert's second wife. His ambitious project was never fully realised, being cut short by his early death in 1930. Passenger services, begun in October 1924 on Saturdays to allow estate workers and their families to go to York market via the North Eastern line at Warthill, were suspended almost at once and goods continued for only a further two years until 30 June 1932. The line was rapidly dismantled and the locomotives scrapped, but there remain in preservation an item from each period of the Sand Hutton line's brief life. The Bassett-Lowke 'Atlantic' *Synolda* from the first line found its way to Ravenglass in Cumbria by way of the miniature railway which operated for many years at Belle Vue Zoo in Manchester and is now restored to working order. One of the coaches from the second line is now restored and working on the Lincolnshire Coast Light Railway at Ingoldmells, near Skegness, having for many years been used as a cricket pavilion.

Scarborough — Whitby

Passenger service withdrawn	8 March 1965	*Stations closed*	*Date of closure*
Distance	23½ miles	Robin Hood's Bay	8 March 1965
Company	Scarborough & Whitby Railway	Hawkser	8 March 1965

Stations closed	*Date of closure*
Scalby *	2 March 1953
Cloughton	8 March 1965
Hayburn Wyke (1st station)	1900
Hayburn Wyke (2nd station) **	8 March 1965
Stainton Dale ***	8 March 1965
Ravenscar ****	8 March 1965
Fyling Hall †	8 March 1965

* Remained open on a restricted basis until final closure in 1964.
** Replaced 1st station on opposite side of level crossing.
*** Originally named Staintondale until 1885 when it was renamed; reverted back to the original name between 1893 and 3 May 1937.
**** Originally named Peak (closed between 6 March 1895 and 1 April 1896) until 1 October 1897.
† Closed between 1 November 1915 and 18 September 1920.

Although it later greatly benefited from the railway, Scarborough was established as a coastal spa resort in the last years of the eighteenth century and the early part of the nineteenth. The fashion for sea bathing among the upper classes grew after George III undertook it as part of his attempted cure for madness; and the closing of continental Europe to British tourists during the Napoleonic wars meant that they looked for diversions at home. The York & North Midland Railway opened its line from York to Scarborough in 1845 and the route from Hull (described in *The Lost Railways of Yorkshire's East Riding*) arrived two years later.

Scalby Station.

Further north, the fishing port and coastal shipping centre of Whitby also gained from the enforced curtailment of European travel in the early nineteenth century. The railway made an early arrival there too, predating the line to Scarborough by ten years and being engineered from Pickering by no less a figure than George Stephenson (see separate section). Having connected both Whitby and Scarborough to the growing national network, attention turned to constructing a direct line between the two, the most likely route hugging the coast in order to avoid climbing up over the moors. Early proposals were made from 1848, but it was 1872 before the first sod of the Scarborough & Whitby Railway's line was cut and another thirteen years before the first train ran, on 16 July 1885, just in time to reap the benefits of the holiday season.

Ravenscar Station.

The line connected with the North Eastern at both ends, but both junctions required trains to reverse in order to get in and out of Scarborough and Whitby stations. Once under way in earnest, trains offered spectacular views as they wound their way along the cliffs, but the going was hard with gradients as steep as 1 in 41 from Scarborough up to the summit of the line at Ravenscar and a climb at an even steeper 1 in 39 in the opposite direction. Rivers running off the moors had cut deep ravines into the coast and none more so than the River Esk as it approached Whitby, necessitating a 915-yard long viaduct at Larpool, high above the Whitby – Pickering line. Once over the viaduct train engines had to run round at Prospect Hill Junction and then descend to Whitby. Even in fair weather the line demanded much of engines and their crews but sea mists and bad weather could make it all but unworkable on occasions.

Wilson Worsdell, the Locomotive Superintendent of the North Eastern went so far as to design a class of engines specially for the line; these were 4-6-0 tank engines, an unusual arrangement in Britain, which were known as the 'W' class, occasioning a range of nicknames, particularly 'Whitby Willies'. It has been argued that they were not equal to the task even after rebuilding as 4-6-2 tanks; they remained at Whitby for a considerable period, though all kinds of engines were pitted against the rigours of the route over the years.

It was the nature of the holiday trade that counted against routes such as this. The summer season was short for most of the nineteenth and early twentieth centuries, mainly only covering July and August; by the time it extended to something like today, particularly in terms of taking out-of-season and extended winter breaks, the British had become enamoured of the attractions and climate of southern Europe. For much of the year lines like the one from Whitby to Scarborough simply marked time, waiting for the crowds to return, and thus became prime targets for the Beeching economies. Despite attempts to cut losses by using multiple-unit diesel trains, the end came for the route on 8 March 1965, though a section was retained from Prospect Hill Junction to Hawkser for possible potash traffic until 1973. Several of the station buildings remain, converted to dwellings, and even though the trains have long gone, it is still possible to travel the route as it has been converted into a cycle and walking path with access from the former stations amongst other points.

Whitby — Saltburn

Passenger service withdrawn	5 May 1958
Distance	38 miles
Company	Whitby, Redcar & Middlesborough Union Railway

Stations closed	Date of closure
Whitby West Cliff	12 June 1961
Sandsend	5 May 1958
Kettleness	5 May 1958
Hinderwell *	5 May 1958
Staithes	5 May 1958
Grinkle **	11 September 1939
Loftus ***	2 May 1960

Stations closed	Date of closure
Skinningrove ****	30 June 1952
Brotton	2 May 1960
North Skelton ***	10 September 1951

* Named 'Hinderwell for Runswick Bay' on some timetables.
** Originally named Easington until 1 April 1904.
*** Originally named Lofthouse until 1 November 1874.
**** Originally named Carlin How until 1 October 1903.
*** Initially closed on 15 January 1951 but subsequently reopened for the summer season on 18 June 1951. Officially closed from 21 January 1964.

North Eastern 0-6-0 No. 2060, built in 1900, with a goods service at Whitby West Cliff Station.

Whitby — Saltburn

Sandsend Station.

The line northwards along the coast from Whitby was a long time in the building, though like the route from Scarborough to Whitby it offered spectacular views to the traveller. Promoted initially by the independent Whitby, Redcar & Middlesborough Union Railway, which obtained parliamentary powers in 1866, construction was slow and in 1875 the company appealed to the North Eastern Railway to take it over and complete the line. Quite what the North Eastern must have thought of its bargain could best be imagined when it discovered not only that the overall standard of work was poor, but sections of the line around Kettleness had fallen into the sea. This resulted in a diversion inland, involving two tunnels between Sandsend and Kettleness, and although the North Eastern made as much speed as it could, construction was slow. The builders worked through the nights and their efforts were illuminated by large bonfires; however, being close to the cliffs the fires were taken by ships at sea to be navigation lights and at least one ran aground, its captain thinking that two fires marked the entrance to the River Esk. Some pointed correspondence between Trinity House and the railway led to the fires being shielded on their seaward side. With all the problems encountered, the intended completion date of July 1881 was extended to December 1883, seventeen years after the WR&MUR had been granted consent to begin work.

Kettleness Station, *c.* **1906.**

Like the Scarborough – Whitby line, the route followed the coast and was obliged to cross a number of deep ravines where rivers ran to the sea. This was done using viaducts of tubular cast iron, the one at Staithes being the largest. One of the viaducts, at Kilton, north of Loftus, suffered the indignity of being buried in an embankment in 1911 after its foundations were undermined by ironstone workings. This section of the line had been built by the Cleveland Railway, which made an end-on junction with the WR&MUR at Lofthouse (as Loftus was named before 1874) and there was a good deal of ironstone mining locally, serving the blast furnaces and ironworks of Middlesborough.

Hinderwell Station.

After opening, the route was worked by the North Eastern and, after 1923, by the London & North Eastern as a continuous line from Saltburn to Scarborough; but in 1933 trains commenced at Middlesborough, running through Guisborough and on to Scarborough. In good weather the coastal views were spectacular but, as on the section south of Whitby, gales and sea fogs could make the journey considerably less attractive. The viaduct at Staithes was equipped with a wind gauge to test when it might be unsafe to cross, a warning bell being provided to alert staff to danger from the elements, although it was said it rang when there was no wind and was silent when it blew! Even when the weather was favourable, trains teetered across the valley at a sedate 20 mph. Kettleness served the village of that name, said to be the most remote in Yorkshire; it also earned a place in literature when Bram Stoker's gothic novel *Dracula* made Kettleness Point the spot where the vampire came ashore at the end of his voyage from Transylvania, though he did not apparently journey onwards by train.

Staithes Station.

The need to reverse at Guisborough, Whitby and Scarborough – a total of six times in 61½ miles – slowed journey times considerably, to say nothing of the fearsome gradients. In 1947 passenger trains calling at all or most stations were allowed between three hours and three hours and ten minutes, at an average speed of around 20mph. Holidaymakers with time to spare might have welcomed such a leisurely progress, but it was hardly a formula for drawing crowds. The line was closed to through traffic from 5 May 1958 – not even waiting until the end of the summer timetable – though the Middlesborough – Guisborough service continued until 2 March 1964 using multiple-unit diesel trains. After closure the viaducts were demolished and this attractive, though troubled, line passed into history.

Stations closed on lines still open to passengers
Darlington — York (East Coast main line)

Stations closed	Date	Stations closed	Date
Cowton	15 September 1958	Alne	5 May 1958
Eryholme *	1 October 1911	Tollerton	1 November 1965
Danby Wiske	15 September 1958	Beningbrough **	15 September 1958
Otterington	15 September 1958		
Sessay	15 September 1958	* Originally named Dalton Junction until 1 May 1901.	
Pilmoor	15 September 1958	** Originally named Shipton until 1 December 1898.	
Raskelf	5 May 1958		

Otterington Station.

Beningbrough Station.

Darlington — York (East Coast main line)

Northallerton — Eaglescliffe *

Stations closed	Date
Brompton	6 September 1965
Welbury	20 September 1954
West Rounton Gates	13 September 1939
Picton	4 January 1960

* The closed station on this line that was in Co. Durham was Yarm.

Brompton Station.

Settle Junction — Carlisle *

Stations closed   *Date*
Garsdale **   4 May 1970

* Closed stations on this line that were in the West Riding were Horton-in-Ribblesdale, Ribblehead and Dent; closed stations in Westmoreland were Kirkby Stephen and Ormside; and closed stations in Cumberland were Long Marton, New Biggin, Culgaith, Langwathby, Little Salkeld, Lazonby & Kirkoswald, Armathwaite, Cotehill and Cumwhinton.

** Originally named Hawes; renamed Hawes Junction & Garsdale on 20 January 1900 and Garsdale from 1 September 1932. The station was reopened from 14 July 1986, although it may have been used for occasional 'Dalesrail' excursions between 1970 and that date.

Garsdale Station, 26 April 1954.

York — Scarborough

Stations closed	Date	Stations closed	Date
Haxby	22 September 1930	Huttons Ambo	22 September 1930
Strensall Halt	22 September 1930	Scarborough Londesborough Road ****	25 August 1963
Strenshall *	22 September 1930		
Flaxton	22 September 1930	* Remained open on a restricted basis until official closure after August 1936.
Barton Hill **	22 September 1930	** Originally named Barton until June 1853.
Kirkham Abbey ***	22 September 1930	*** Originally named Kirkham until 1 June 1875.
Castle Howard	22 September 1930	**** Originally named Scarborough Excursion until 1 June 1933.

Strenshall Station.

York — Scarborough

Flaxton Station.

Kirkham Abbey Station.

York — Scarborough